DAVID MICHAEL

BIG, BOLD, BIBLICAL PRAYERS FOR THE NEXT GENERATION

Truth:78

Big, Bold, Biblical Prayers for the Next Generation
by David Michael

Copyright © 2018 Next Generation Resources, Inc. Illustrations Truth78.
All rights reserved. No part of this publication may be reproduced in any form
without written permission from Truth78.

Published in the United States by Truth78.

All Scripture quotations, unless otherwise noted, are from The Holy Bible,
English Standard Version® (ESV®), copyright © 2001 by Crossway,
a publishing ministry of Good News Publishers. Used by permission.
All rights reserved.

ISBN: 978-0-9969870-7-3

Rev. 10.18

Truth:78 / Equipping the Next Generations
to Know, Honor, and Treasure God

Truth78.org · info@Truth78.org · 877.400.1414 · @Truth78org

Contents

Will you pray big, bold, biblical prayers for the next generation?

- Access resources designed to help you share this with others.

- Download a digital copy.

- Order a print copy (including bulk orders).

- Join a community committed to praying big, bold, biblical prayers for the next generation.

- Sign up to receive encouragement and examples for big, bold, biblical prayer.

Visit Truth78.org/prayer

Introduction

As I was tracking down source information for one of the quotes in this booklet, I noticed the preface in a book I was citing. I smiled when I read it because I appreciate C. H. Spurgeon's sense of humor, and especially because I could identify with what he was saying.

> I have no idea of what I am expected to say in a preface, and I am of the opinion that a book is better without an appendage usually so unmeaning. I will, however, make one or two faithful declarations which may, perhaps, shield me from the reader's wrath, should he find my work of less value than he expected. Never was there a book written amid more incessant toil…Writing is to me the work of a slave. It is a delight, a joy, a rapture to talk out one's thoughts in words that flash upon the mind at the instant when they are required; but it is pure drudgery to sit still and groan for thoughts and words without succeeding in obtaining them.[1]

For me, it has only taken a few days of "groaning" and "rapture," "drudgery" and "delight" to put words to thoughts that have been forming and simmering for more than a year. By the summer of 2017, it seemed as though the organization that is the tangible expression of my heart and vision for the faith of the next generation had reached its lowest point since 1998, when Children Desiring God was founded. In the midst of all the planning and preparation for the transition to our new name, some of us were wondering if there would ever be a Truth78.

I will offer a few more details later in this booklet, but here I would like to make one "faithful declaration," perhaps to "shield me from the reader's wrath," but mainly to help the reader understand what this small booklet represents for Truth78. By

---

[1] C. H. Spurgeon. *The Saint and His Savior: or, The Progress of the Soul in the Knowledge of Jesus.* (New York: Sheldon, Blakeman, and Company, 1857), v.

the end of 2017, sorrow melted away, hope revived, fresh vision came, and an all-time low was transformed into one of the most exciting times to be part of this ministry.

This transformation coincided with a change of emphasis in our prayers. We had been focusing our prayers on our need for increased sales and the development of our donor base. It is not that we were wrong to ask for our sales to increase and our fundraising efforts to succeed, but that the declining sales and need for funds seemed more urgent to me than our mission—to faithfully declare as far and as wide as we can to the next generations "the glorious deeds of the LORD, and his might, and the wonders that he has done."[2] For more than two decades we had been committed to doing this through the God-ordained institutions that He has established, namely the church and the home.

> **"This project was born out of an earnest desire to see what God might be pleased to do if 10,000 or more people invest time at least once a week to pray a big, bold, biblical prayer from their hearts for the next generation."**
>
> **—DAVID MICHAEL**

But here I was, feeling more desperate about the circumstances that were prompting desperate prayers, rather than the massively more significant concerns for the faith of the next generation.

The change came when we shifted our attention and our desperation toward the greater concerns and focused less on the immediate financial challenges we were facing. When we changed the way we prayed, our hope revived, our faith increased, and we fretted less about finances.

I want to be careful to emphasize that this is not a playbook for successful fundraising. The fact that our financial situation improved and fresh excitement for the future came is owing to

[2]Psalm 78:4

nothing other than the grace and undeserved kindness of God. Please don't interpret this as, "If you pray big, bold, biblical prayers, your plans will succeed." Instead, know that if we pray big, bold, biblical prayers for the next generation, what can happen is that the greater cause will matter more to us than the lesser. We will understand that the lesser causes, like the success of Truth78, are there to serve the greater. If, in the wisdom of God, the greater cause could flourish without Truth78, then we rest in the wisdom that is infinitely greater than ours.

To be honest, the push to get this booklet done now is because we are into the final quarter of the year, which expert fundraisers say is the best time to ask people for money. We feel an urgency because of significant financial challenges and milestones we are eager to reach in order to pursue the mission about which we are increasingly excited.

But we are trying to put our money where our mouth is. We want to invest our time in this strategic season of the year to mobilize God's people to pray big, bold, biblical prayers for the next generation. This project was born out of an earnest desire to see what God might be pleased to do if 10,000 or more people invest time at least once a week to pray a big, bold, biblical prayer from their hearts for the next generation.

If the Lord is pleased to answer such prayers, we believe that Truth78 will have what is needed for as long as God is pleased to use our efforts to accomplish the great cause. May this little booklet be of some help to all who read it, and inspire 10,000 more to pursue the everlasting joy of the next generation on our knees in big, bold, biblical prayer.

The Prayers of this Generation Matter to the Next

Over the years of our ministry, my wife Sally and I have taught various classes and seminars that offer vision and practical strategies for Christian parents who are committed to faithfully raising their children in the "instruction of the Lord."[3] There is a tension we often feel when teaching on the subject of faith and children. The tension is between the responsibility Christian parents have to give their children what matters most and the reality that, apart from Christ, parents have no power to ensure that their children embrace what ultimately matters most to them and to us. There is no way parents can escape responsibility for nurturing the faith of their children, and there is no way to escape the reality that their children will only be saved by the grace of God through faith in Jesus Christ.[4] The most biblical vision, the best parenting strategies, and the most comprehensive Deuteronomy 6:7-9 instruction in the Christian faith does not guarantee that children will be born again and that parents will experience the joy of seeing them walk in the Truth. Saving faith for any child "is the gift of God, not a result of works, so that no one [no parent, no pastor, no grandparent, no Sunday school teacher] may boast."[5]

We have encouraged parents to heed their biblical responsibility, and offered tools and support to raise their children in the faith. We have also encouraged parents with the hope-giving assurance that God rules over the hearts of their children[6] and can transform the most stubborn and spiritually resistant heart into a soul that pants for Christ "as a deer pants for flowing streams."[7]

[3]Ephesians 6:4
[4]Ephesians 2:8-9
[5]Ibid.
[6]Proverbs 21:1
[7]Psalm 42:1

We challenge parents to work out the salvation of their children "with fear and trembling"[8] and, at the same time, to hold fast to the assurance that God is at work in them and in their children "both to will and to work for his good pleasure."[9]

God's unstoppable purposes for our children and our inescapable responsibility to raise them in the faith come together in prayer. The Apostle Paul stuns us at the beginning of Ephesians by assuring us that every true child of God was chosen in Christ to be "holy and blameless," and this was "before the foundation of the world...predestined...for adoption...according to the purpose of his will, to the praise of his glorious grace."[10] And yet, having just affirmed this reality for every believer, Paul still prayed that their hearts would be enlightened,[11] and he bowed his knees so that (among other reasons) "Christ may dwell in [their] hearts through faith."[12]

Even more stunning are Jesus' words to Peter the night before He was crucified: "Satan demanded to have you, that he might sift you like wheat, but I have prayed for you that your faith may not fail."[13] Isn't that amazing? Jesus, the Son of God, who sustains the universe by the word of His power, felt compelled to pray that Peter's faith would not fail after He had declared with absolute authority that this same man was the rock on which "I will build my church, and the gates of hell shall not prevail against it."[14]

In 2003, George Barna published the results of an extensive study that I have found useful for inspiring prayer for the next generation. In this book,[15] Barna helps us assess the spiritual influence we are having on the next generations and makes an interesting observation. He notes that *churches with the most effective and fruitful ministries to children were also churches that were the most serious about prayer.*

---

[8]Philippians 2:12
[9]Philippians 2:13
[10]Ephesians 1:4-6
[11]Ephesians 1:18
[12]Ephesians 3:17
[13]Luke 22:31-32
[14]Matthew 16:18
[15]George Barna. *Transforming Children into Spiritual Champions: Why Children Should Be Your Church's #1 Priority.* (Raleigh, N.C.: Regal Books, a division of Gospel Light, 2003), 102-104.

He found the most productive children's ministries have five areas of prayer focus. In summary, they are:

1. Teachers praying for each of their students on a regular basis.
2. Teachers praying as a team, usually on a weekly basis, along with other staff and church leaders in the children's ministry.
3. Intercessors volunteering to faithfully pray for the teachers and students.
4. The entire congregation frequently praying for children's ministry.
5. Parents praying during prayer times organized by the church, and in connection with prayer partners.

> **"Prayer works in these churches because the body of believers shares God's heartbeat about the importance of children and believes that prayer makes a difference in people's lives. The result is obvious..."**
>
> **—GEORGE BARNA**

Barna says, "These churches are unusually effective, I believe, because they constantly beg God to bless the work related to the moral and spiritual maturation of their congregation's young people...Prayer works in these churches because the body of believers shares God's heartbeat about the importance of children and believes that prayer makes a difference in people's lives. The result is obvious..."[16]

Another source for prayer inspiration comes from Reverend William Scribner, an American pastor who published in 1873, *An Appeal to Parents to Pray Continually for the Welfare and Salvation of Their Children.*[17] The book is divided into two parts that offer practical and biblical reasons why we should pray for our children's salvation and for their welfare. Just reviewing

---

[16]George Barna. *Transforming Children into Spiritual Champions: Why Children Should Be Your Church's #1 Priority.* (Raleigh, N.C.: Regal Books, a Division of Gospel Light of Ventura California, 2003), 102-104.

[17]Rev. William Scribner. *Pray for Your Children, or An Appeal to Parents to Pray Continually for the Welfare and Salvation of Their Children.* (Philadelphia, Penn.: Presbyterian Board of Publication, 1873), https://archive.org/details/prayforyourchild00scri/page/n0 (accessed 10/11/18).

the headings for each of Scribner's sections provides us with substantial encouragement to pray for the next generation:

Praying for Your Children's Salvation

1. Their salvation is so great a prize that it is worth all the pains which your prayer to secure it for them may cost you.
2. Few will pray for them if you do not.
3. No one else can pray for them as you do.
4. Your omitting to do so will be perilous to them and to you.
5. You will then find it easier to perform other parental duties, which God has ordained as a means to their salvation.
6. Prayer alone can call into exercise that divine power on their behalf, which is absolutely necessary in order that the prayers which you may employ for their salvation may not be used in vain.
7. By their salvation, granted in answer to your prayers, your Savior will be glorified.

Praying for Your Children's Welfare

1. You may then expect, as a result of your prayers, that the power of God will counteract in some measure the evil you have done them.
2. There will be critical periods in their lives when, without your incessant prayers, they may be left to act most unwisely, if not disastrously.
3. It will lead you to a better understanding of them.
4. It will increase your holy desires for them.
5. No other means will be so effectual in enabling you to overcome the difficulty you experience in talking with them on religious subjects.
6. You will thereby secure for them God's aid in the efforts they may make to yield to you in obedience.
7. Other parents seeing your example, may be led to imitate you.

8. *They will often, should they continue in the world, have their times of need when the power of God alone can avail to help them.*

Bottom line—prayer matters! It matters to us. It matters to our children. It matters to every generation until Jesus comes. It matters because God is pleased to accomplish His unstoppable purposes through the prayers of His people.

Big, Bold, Biblical Prayers

An effort to inspire people to pray big, bold, biblical prayers for the next generation requires an explanation of what we mean by "big," "bold," and "biblical." In these opening paragraphs, I want to offer some personal history, which I hope will provide a context for understanding these ideas, and for appreciating the undeserved grace of God that awakened my passion for praying this way.

I have had the privilege of serving as a pastor in two churches led by men with extraordinary preaching gifts. Consequently (and thankfully), I have had more opportunities to pray publicly than to preach.

My first opportunity came when I was assigned to pray the pastoral prayer on Father's Day in 1986. The prayer was about five minutes long, and it took me several hours to prepare. I had six more opportunities that year, each taking a significant amount of time to prepare. In the 10 years that followed, I was assigned a pastoral prayer at least once a month. Eventually, I was able to reduce my preparation time but, to this day, it can still take two hours to prepare.

Although I had been praying to God all my life, it was different praying in front of several hundred people. Undoubtedly, there was some fear of man going on in my heart, but mainly I was feeling the weight of responsibility to pray on behalf of these people. I had been gripped by a sentence underlined and marked with triple stars in my copy of *Lectures to My Students* in which Spurgeon offers 16 pages of instruction how to pray publicly and says:

> *...draw the whole congregation with you up to the throne of God...by the power of the Holy Spirit resting on you, you*

express the desires and thoughts of everyone present, and
stand as the one voice for the hundreds of beating hearts
which are glowing with fervor before the throne of God[18]

That sentence helped explain why the assignment to pray a pastoral prayer seemed so weighty to me. Much of my preparation time was spent trying to discern what would be on the hearts of the people as I stood to pray, and then trying to put words together in a way that would be concise and meaningful, and best express our affections for God, our sorrow for sin, the burdens we were carrying, and the longings of our hearts.

Incidentally, no one helped me grow in the discipline of public prayer more than Spurgeon, which explains the number of quotes I have from him in this chapter. Shortly after being asked to pray my first public pastoral prayer, I acquired a copy of the 1906 edition of his pulpit prayers. These prayers have often stirred my soul as much as, if not more than his sermons. In fact, in the introduction to the collection, the compiler wrote, "It was memorable to hear this incomparable divine [Spurgeon] when he preached. It was often more memorable to hear him pray."[19] American evangelist D. L. Moody confirmed this when spoke in the Metropolitan Tabernacle in October 1892: "He recalled an earlier visit twenty-five years previously. He had come four thousand miles, he said, to hear C. H. Spurgeon, but what impressed him most was not the sermon, nor the singing of the great congregation, but Spurgeon's prayer."[20] The collection of his pulpit prayers and his practical instruction in *Lectures to My Students*, and at least one of his sermons, "The Golden Key of Prayer"[21] have been invaluable resources.

For more than two decades, my responsibilities have included oversight of our child dedication services, each of which usually ends with a pastoral prayer. With Spurgeon's words still ringing

---

[18]C. H. Spurgeon. *Lectures to My Students: Complete & Unabridged. Ministry Resources Library.* (Grand Rapids, Mich.: Zondervan Publishing House, 1989), 60.
[19]Ibid.
[20]Ibid.
[21]C. H. Spurgeon. "The Golden Key of Prayer," Sermon #619, as published in *Metropolitan Tabernacle Pulpit Volume 11*, delivered on Sunday morning, March 12, 1865 at the Metropolitan Tabernacle, Newington, London, England.

in my ears, these prayers are influenced by the hopes and desires that many Christian parents have for their children. They also reflect the responsibility the congregation has for influencing the faith of these children and a biblical vision for the next generation. Preparing these prayers at least four times a year has been good for me. Putting words to the desires of my heart for the next generation and expressing them to God has influenced my personal prayer life and the way I pray for my own children and grandchildren. I've also discovered the value that big, bold, biblical prayers have for cultivating a vision for the next generation and engaging the heart of the congregation for that vision. I am also confident that God is attentive to thoughtful prayers that flow from the heart rather than a heap of "empty phrases"[22] from hearts that are far from Him.[23]

Out of this experience came important thoughts that have influenced the development of this resource for Truth78. Somewhere along the way it occurred to me that if I am investing a couple hours preparing to pray to God in front of a few hundred people, should I not be at least that prepared whenever I come before the Lord in prayer? If I am trembling at the thought of being "one voice for the hundreds of beating hearts,"[24] should I not be trembling at least that much at the thought of coming into the presence of the Almighty, where gathered before His throne are "creatures and the elders [and] angels, numbering myriads of myriads and thousands of thousands, saying with a loud voice, 'Worthy is the Lamb who was slain, to receive power and wealth and wisdom and might and honor and glory and blessing'"?[25]

I thank God that in Christ we have an "advocate with the Father,"[26] "who is at the right hand of God, who indeed is interceding for us."[27] Likewise, I thank God that "the Spirit helps us in our weakness. For we do not know what to pray for as we ought, but the Spirit himself intercedes for us with groanings too deep for

[22]Matthew 6:7
[23]Isaiah 29:13
[24]C. H. Spurgeon. Lectures to My Students: Complete & Unabridged. Ministry Resources Library. (Grand Rapids, Mich.: Zondervan Publishing House, 1989), 60.
[25]Revelation 5:11-12
[26]1 John 2:1
[27]Romans 8:34

words."[28] I will forever give thanks for the "Spirit of adoption as sons, by whom we cry, 'Abba! Father!'"[29] Would we not consider it strange if any child felt the need to spend several hours preparing before talking to his dad? Doesn't it follow that it we should consider it equally strange for those who are truly "adopted as sons" and given blood-bought freedom to come to the infinitely holy God as "Abba Father" to spend several hours preparing to come to Him in prayer?

> "What might God be pleased to do if His people come to Him with big, bold, biblical prayers of faith? I hope we will soon find out."
>
> —DAVID MICHAEL

In one sense, I would not only consider it strange, but also an offense to the cross if a child of God felt that anything more than our identity in Christ is needed to commune with the Living God. However, does it really honor the one who paid with His blood to give us access to the Father, if we give no thought to aligning our desires with His and considering His promises so that we can ask according to His Word? Spurgeon went on to emphasize to his students the importance of preparing their hearts to pray, which "consists in the solemn consideration beforehand of the importance of prayer, meditation upon the needs of men's souls, and a remembrance of the promises which we are to plead; and thus coming before the Lord with a petition written on the tables of the heart. This is surely better than coming to God at random, rushing before the throne at haphazard, without a definite errand or desire."[30]

The needs of those in the next generation, the challenges they face, and the opportunities before them are great. What might God be pleased to do if His people come to Him with big, bold, biblical prayers of faith? I hope we will soon find out.

---

[28]Romans 8:26

[29]Romans 8:15

[30]C. H. Spurgeon. *Lectures to My Students: Complete & Unabridged. Ministry Resources Library.* (Zondervan, Mich.: Zondervan Publishing House, 1989), 68.

Big Prayers

Big prayers are not necessarily long prayers. They are big in scope. Jesus' words at the end of Matthew 6 suggest this. After pointing us to the "birds of the air" that "neither sow nor reap nor gather into barns," and the "lilies of the field" that "neither toil nor spin," Jesus says, "Therefore do not be anxious, saying, 'What shall we eat?' or 'What shall we drink?' or 'What shall we wear?'... But seek first the kingdom of God and his righteousness, and all these things will be added to you."[31]

It would follow from this passage that when we pray for the next generation, our first prayers should be for the greater things—the big things—the Kingdom-sized things, as we trust God for the lesser things. This does not suggest we should neglect praying for the smaller things, but rather we should prioritize our prayers toward the greater. In the example He gave earlier in Matthew 6, Jesus taught us to first pray, "Your kingdom come, your will be done, on earth as it is in heaven," and then He prayed "Give us this day our daily bread."[32]

When praying for the next generation, I want to urge us to invest heavily in praying the big prayers that clearly align with God's Kingdom purposes for the next generation, though we are not wrong in asking God for small things on behalf of our children.

It is certainly fitting to ask our heavenly Father to give our children a fun day, help them learn to share with their siblings, do well on their math test, heal them when they are sick, encourage them when they are discouraged, provide for their education, give them a godly spouse, and provide us with lots of grandchildren! However, too often, our prayers for the next generation are limited to our concern for the lesser things, and we neglect to pray God's greater purposes for our children and their generation, and the generations to come.

Notice Jesus told us that when we seek first God's Kingdom and His righteousness (big things), that "all these things" (small

---

[31]Matthew 6:26, 28, 31, 33
[32]Matthew 6:10-11

17

things like food and clothes) "will be added to you." When we pray big prayers for the next generation, the lesser things are often included.

King Solomon discovered this when he asked God for an understanding mind to govern the people of God with wisdom and justice, and to discern good and evil. "It pleased the Lord that Solomon had asked this. And God said to him, 'Because you have asked this, and have not asked for yourself long life or riches or the life of your enemies, but have asked for yourself understanding to discern what is right, behold...I give you a wise and discerning mind...I give you also what you have not asked, both riches and honor, so that no other king shall compare with you, all your days.'"[33]

Asking our Father in heaven to let the hearts of my children be glad and their whole beings rejoice,[34] and to give them the "fullness of joy" in His presence and eternal pleasures "at [His] right hand"[35] can include the desire for our children to have a fun day. Asking God to equip my children "with everything good" to do His will, and to work in them "that which is pleasing in his sight"[36] encompasses the desire that they would share with their siblings, and more! Having a child do well on a math test can be important, but that importance fades compared with the importance of our children having "all spiritual wisdom and understanding, so as to walk in a manner worthy of the Lord."[37] If I am earnestly seeking God to give my child all spiritual wisdom, doing well on the math test seems less urgent. In the end, what will make us happier—a child who is good at math, or a child who is walking in a manner worthy of the Lord? It is true that one desire does not necessarily rule out the other, and it does not displease the Lord to ask Him for help on the math test. My concern is that we plead for help with the math test while neglecting to plead for something massively more important, and more explicitly aligned with the will of God for our children.

---

[33] 1 Kings 3:11-13
[34] Psalm 16:9
[35] Psalm 16:11
[36] Hebrews 13:21
[37] Colossians 1:9-10

18

Even though we ask for a lot when we ask for grace to faithfully declare "the glorious deeds of the LORD, and his might"[38] and "the whole counsel of God"[39] to our children so that the next generation might know the Truth, even the children yet unborn, that they would arise and tell them to their children so that they should set their hope in God,[40] we can pray with more boldness and confidence because we know that what we ask clearly accords with God's will more than many of the smaller things.

When we focus on the big prayers, we are more likely to recognize that God addresses the smaller concerns in light of His greater purposes. Paul clearly trusted Christ to supply every need (including daily bread) "according to his riches in glory in Christ Jesus,"[41] and yet seven verses earlier he tells us he "learned the secret of facing plenty and hunger, abundance and need."[42] In the previous chapter in Philippians, Paul revealed that the secret to facing hunger was to seek first the greater things like "the surpassing worth of knowing Christ Jesus."[43] He was content to be without a lesser thing like food that he might "gain Christ and be found in him," and have a righteousness that "comes through faith in Christ," and that he may know Christ and "the power of his resurrection, and may share his sufferings, becoming like him in his death, that by any means possible [he] may attain the resurrection from the dead."[44]

In other words, when we are passionately seeking and praying for the greater things, we are more inclined to trust the faithfulness and wisdom of God when the outcome of the lesser things is disappointing. It may be that failing a math test is one of the means God will use to grant your child "all spiritual wisdom and understanding, so as to walk in a manner worthy of the Lord."[45]

For more than 20 years, I have overseen ministries for children in the church. Almost without exception, we have approached each

---

[38]Psalm 78:4
[39]Acts 20:27
[40]Psalm 78:4-7
[41]Philippians 4:19
[42]Philippians 4:12
[43]Philippians 3:8
[44]Philippians 3:8-11
[45]Colossians 1:9-10

school year with significant volunteer needs. August of 2017 at College Park Church was no exception. We were two weeks from our fall program launch, and we still needed 130 volunteers.

Also, for more than two decades I have been providing leadership for a ministry devoted to equipping the church and parents with resources for the discipleship of the next generations. For years, God sustained that ministry through sales of these resources. But in the summer of 2017, we experienced a serious drop in sales that threatened the viability of the ministry. This chapter is the fruit of that difficult summer.

As we considered the future, we were confident that God had not promised increasing revenue and the long-term viability of our ministry any more than He had promised College Park Church 130 workers by August 20. There was definitely no harm in asking for such things, but we decided to concentrate our prayers on the greater things. We prayed that Jesus would build His church, and that the gates of hell would not prevail against His unstoppable purposes. We prayed that our generation would be faithful in declaring the glorious deeds of the LORD to the next. We prayed that we would have all we needed to faithfully and fruitfully impart to our children the whole counsel of God. We concentrated on seeking first God's Kingdom purposes for the next generation, and we decided not to ask but to trust Him for the lesser things like revenue and volunteers.

Looking back on the fourth quarter of 2017, we thank God for providing enough volunteers for College Park ministries, as well as providing a slight increase in sales for Truth78 (then

> "We expect that the needs and challenges will always be there, but by God's grace our most earnest and most desperate prayers will be the 'big prayers' for greater things that conform to God's heart and His unstoppable purposes for the next generation."
>
> —DAVID MICHAEL

called Children Desiring God). God also brought us something completely unexpected that quarter. Some of us will remember it as "the December miracle" when, beyond what we asked or imagined, God breathed fresh life and vision into our little ministry as we transitioned from Children Desiring God to Truth78. A year later, we still needed volunteers at College Park. A year later, we are still facing significant challenges at Truth78. We expect that the needs and challenges will always be there, but by God's grace our most earnest and most desperate prayers will be the "big prayers" for greater things that conform to God's heart and His unstoppable purposes for the next generation.

Bold Prayers

Bold prayers of the sort that I have in mind for the next generation rise from unwavering confidence in three realities.

1. God is who He says He is. He is infinite and perfect in all His attributes. He knows everything. He can do anything. He can be everywhere all the time. He doesn't sleep or slumber. He never grows weary or faint. There are no limits to His power, and nothing is above His dominion and authority. He is always watching, and He is always attentive. Everything good that we can ask of God, He is able to do. Therefore, we can ask with bold confidence in Him.

2. God always keeps His promises and accomplishes all that He sets out to do. Therefore, we can boldly ask Him to do what He has promised to do and to accomplish His purposes that were established before the foundation of the world.

   It is difficult to be bold in prayer when we have no assurance that our prayers align with His promises and His purpose. I can't pray boldly that my child will do well on his math test because, as I've already noted, it may be that failing the math test is more perfectly aligned with God's will for my child. I could, however, boldly pray that the outcome of the test would have its sanctifying effect on my child because Paul states explicitly that God wills our sanctification.[46]

Although it would have been appropriate to ask, I could not boldly pray that my father would be healed from cancer, because there was nothing promised or willed by God that gave me confidence that my dad would be healed this side of heaven. But I was able to pray boldly that the cancer would not take him one day sooner, or delay him one day longer, than what God had ordained for his life.[47] I could pray that his faith would not fail,[48] and that the tested genuineness of his faith would be found "to result in praise and glory and honor at the revelation of Jesus Christ."[49]

Even Jesus could not boldly pray "let this cup pass from me," but He could pray with absolute confidence and boldness "not as I will, but as you will"[50] and "glorify your Son that the Son may glorify you."[51]

In the summer of 2017, we had no assurance that Children Desiring God would survive the year, or that there would ever be a Truth78. But we were assured with great confidence that the next generation would know the glorious deeds of the LORD. We could ask with confidence for grace to be faithful in making Him known to the next generation. We could boldly pray that "every knee" would bow and "every tongue confess that Jesus Christ is Lord, to the glory of God the Father."[52] We knew we were praying according to His will when we asked God to grant that the next generation would be "rooted and grounded in love," and "have strength to comprehend with all the saints what is the breadth and length and height and depth, and to know the love of Christ that surpasses knowledge, that [they] may be filled with all the fullness of God."[53]

---

[46] 1 Thessalonians 4:3
[47] Psalm 139:16
[48] Luke 22:32
[49] 1 Peter 1:7
[50] Matthew 26:39
[51] John 17:1
[52] Philippians 2:10-11
[53] Ephesians 3:17-19

Not every bold prayer for the next generation rises from absolute certainty that it accords with God's sovereign purposes. I have often prayed, for example, "that every child who is known and loved by someone in this room would be saved—that not one would be lost." This big and bold prayer is linked to the Truth that God "is able to save to the uttermost,"[54] and He does not will "that any should perish,"[55] and that "everyone who calls on the name of the Lord will be saved."[56] I pray boldly knowing that God is moved by the prayers of His people,[57] and some will be saved in response to the bold prayers of His people. I pray boldly because Paul's "heart's desire and prayer to God for [Israel]" was that they may be saved.[58] And I pray boldly and in accord with God's will for His people with confidence that the Judge of all the earth will do what is right even if, in the end, some of the children I pray for perish in unbelief.

3. Bold prayers are only possible "in Christ Jesus our Lord."[59] Paul tells us, "we have boldness and access with confidence through our faith in him."[60] Because we have such "a great high priest," the writer of Hebrews encourages us to approach the throne of grace with confidence, so "that we may receive mercy and find grace to help in time of need."[61] Godly boldness in prayer comes from the awareness that we have no merit of our own.

Apart from Christ, we are cut off without hope, and without God in the world. Apart from Christ, we can make no appeal and have no access. Apart from Christ, we would be incinerated in the presence of God.

The reason these writers had to urge us to boldly and confidently approach the throne of grace is that we are naturally and understandably cautious when we rightly understand our

---

[54] Hebrews 7:25
[55] 2 Peter 3:9
[56] Romans 10:13
[57] 2 Chronicles 7:14
[58] Romans 10:1
[59] Ephesians 3:11
[60] Ephesians 3:12
[61] Hebrews 4:14, 16

sin-contaminated nature apart from Christ, and consider the glory and majesty and dominion and authority of God, before whom seraphim and cherubim and elders and the heavenly host bow before the throne in endless worship of the great I AM. And yet, Christ is able to present us "blameless before the presence of his glory with great joy."[62] So, with boldness, we can make our appeal through Christ.

Not all boldness in prayer is necessarily godly boldness that pleases God. Ungodly boldness does not rise from humble dependence on Christ but from prideful confidence in who we think we are. Namaan serves as a good example. His boldness when he first approached Elisha was based on his position as a commander of the Syrian army and who he was as a man, mighty in valor and great in wealth.

> **"boldness that springs from grace and is the work of the Spirit, [is] not the boldness of a rebel who carries a brazen front in the presence of his offended king, but the boldness of the child who fears because he loves, and loves because he fears."**
>
> **—C.H. SPURGEON**

Spurgeon clarifies that "boldness that springs from grace and is the work of the Spirit, [is] not the boldness of a rebel who carries a brazen front in the presence of his offended king, but the boldness of the child who fears because he loves, and loves because he fears. Never fall into a vainglorious style of impertinent address to God; he is not to be assailed as an antagonist, but entreated with as our Lord and God. Humble and lowly let us be in spirit, and so let us pray."[63]

Boldness in prayer for the next generation must not rise from our Christ-less self-confidence. The reason we come boldly

---

[62] Jude 1:24

[63] C. H. Spurgeon. *Lectures to My Students: Complete & Unabridged. Ministry Resources Library.* (Grand Rapids, Mich.: Zondervan Publishing House, 1989), 57.

to the throne of grace is not because we are good parents or grandparents faithfully instructing our children in the faith and raising them in the discipline and instruction of the Lord. Similarly, my bold confidence in prayer for the next generation is not rooted in my identity as a pastor, or my years of service in ministry to parents, children, and youth, or my involvement in an organization founded on the Psalm 78:7 passion for the next generation to set their hope in God. Bold prayers for the next generation arise from our confidence in Christ and all that He is for those who belong to Him.

I doubt anyone has been more confident in Christ than Paul. We can tell this by the boldness of his prayers. As he concludes the third chapter of Ephesians, Paul bowed his "knees before the Father, from whom every family in heaven and on earth is named,"[64] and prayed this bold and glorious prayer "that according to the riches of his glory" God would grant that these people Paul loved would be "strengthened with power through his Spirit in [their] inner being, so that Christ might dwell in [their] hearts through faith," and that they, "being rooted and grounded in love, may have strength to comprehend with all the saints what is the breadth and length and height and depth, and to know the love of Christ that surpasses knowledge, that [they] may be filled with all the fullness of God" through "him who is able to do far more abundantly than all that we ask or think, according to the power at work within us, to whom be glory in the church and in Christ Jesus throughout all generations, forever and ever. Amen."[65]

Biblical Prayers

Biblical prayers for the next generation resonate with the hearts of God's people and often inspire vision and hope as we pray them. In John 15, Jesus makes an important connection between His Word and our prayers, as well as a breathtaking offer. "If you abide in me, and my words abide in you, ask whatever you wish, and it will be done for you."[66] Our big prayers for the next

---

[64]Ephesians 3:14-15
[65]Ephesians 3:16-21
[66]John 15:7

generation and the boldness we have in praying them stand on Truth revealed in the Bible. I am convinced that one of the ways the Holy Spirit has already helped us for those times when "we do not know what to pray for as we ought"[67] is by giving us a Bible filled with words of Truth and glorious promises that we can pray.

Once again, Spurgeon's words to his students are instructive: "Be constant in reading the Word and meditation thereon...The sure words of Scripture are the footsteps of Jesus imprinted on the soil of mercy—follow the track and find Him. The promises are cards of admission not only to the throne room, the mercy-seat, and the audience-chamber, but to the very heart of Jesus. Look aloft to the sky of revelation, and thou wilt find a constellation of promises which shall guide thine eye to the Star of Bethlehem. Above all, cry aloud when you read a promise—Remember Thy word unto Thy servant, on which Thou has caused me to hope."[68]

The reason D. L. Moody and countless others were so moved by Spurgeon's prayers had less to do with Spurgeon and more to do with the fact that his prayers were so saturated with the Word of God.

Many years ago, our pastoral team—about eight of us at the time—was traveling together for a two-day retreat. On our way out of town, we decided to stop at the hospital and pray for one of our members. When we arrived, we realized there were more of us than could fit in the room, so John Piper and one or two others went in to pray while the rest of us waited in the hall outside the room and across from the nurses station. Since the door was closed, we couldn't hear what was being said. After about five minutes, one of the nurses came out of the room and said to her colleague at the station, "It sounds like God is praying in there!"

As with Spurgeon, I witnessed the power and influence of Bible-saturated prayers serving alongside one of the most Bible-saturated men I know. I have no doubt that the reason John Piper sounded like God to this woman when he prayed was because he

---

[67]Romans 8:26

[68]C. H. Spurgeon. *The Saint and His Savior: or, The Progress of the Soul in the Knowledge of Jesus.* (New York: Sheldon, Blakeman, and Company, 1857), 147.

was praying God's Word. Prayers shaped and influenced by the Word of God have a tone of authority and strength that our own words—even thoughtful and well-articulated words—do not have.

Even when praying with no one but God listening, my hope and confidence rise when I am praying the Word of God. Praying with my Bible open and letting prayer rise from reading God's Word strengthens my faith. I have also discovered that having portions of the Bible memorized gives substance to both my private and public prayer. Also, since I am not naturally articulate, it is so helpful, especially in those spontaneous moments when I am called upon to pray, to have the words of my prayer flow from something that I have memorized.

By encouraging biblical prayers, I am not suggesting we should just open our Bibles and start quoting verses. When we abide in Christ and in His Word, our biblically informed, biblically minded, biblically shaped prayers will come naturally without necessarily quoting any particular portion of Scripture.

In an effort to pray "biblical prayers," I sometimes hear people say to the Lord something like, "I thank You for Your Word that says the fruit of the Spirit is love, joy, peace, patience, kindness, goodness, faithfulness, gentleness, and self-control. I thank You, Father, that against such things there is no law."[69] Taking such a prayer at face value, this person is expressing gratitude to God for a particular portion of Scripture that is meaningful. There is certainly nothing wrong with expressing gratitude to God in this way. Sometimes, however, I sense the person is saying less to God in those moments and more to the people who are listening.

Spurgeon warns his young students to "pray to God right through the prayer, and never fall to talking or preaching—much less, as some do—scolding and grumbling."[70] "Let the Lord alone be the object of your prayers. Beware of having an eye to the auditors; beware of becoming rhetorical to please the listeners. Prayer must not be turned into an oblique sermon."[71]

---

[69]Galatians 5:22-23
[70]C. H. Spurgeon. *Lectures to My Students: Complete & Unabridged. Ministry Resources Library.* (Grand Rapids, Mich.: Zondervan Publishing House, 1989), 58.
[71]Ibid, 55.

27

Recently, I was praying with a father concerning a particularly difficult and defiant child. We spent an hour considering various strategies we could apply and, at the end of the conversation, we prayed. As I was praying, Galatians 5:22-23 came to mind and I prayed something like, "have mercy on this boy, and by the power of your Holy Spirit grant that love, joy, peace, patience, kindness, goodness, faithfulness, gentleness, and especially self-control dominate his life and character and personality." As I began listing the fruit of the Spirit, the dad with quiet earnestness said, "Yes Lord, please!" In that moment, there was an immediate connection. Those familiar words triggered a response from this dad and united his heart with mine in a shared desire for his son to come under the influence of the Spirit.

It is important to note that we must be as committed to the faithful use and application of the Bible in our prayers as we are in our preaching. Because prayer seems so personal and intimate, we are more likely to overlook or neglect the misapplication of Scripture or serious doctrinal blunders that we would never tolerate in preaching. The abuse of Scripture in public prayer was an obvious issue in Spurgeon's day and a serious concern for him. He invested almost five full pages to exhorting his students to be faithful interpreters of the Bible, even in their prayers. After giving examples of the misapplication of Scripture or Scripture mixed with extra-biblical quotations in prayer, Spurgeon stated that "the miserable conglomeration of perversions of Scripture, uncouth similes, and ridiculous metaphors, constitute a sort of spiritual slang, the offspring of unholy ignorance, unmanly imitation, or graceless hypocrisy; they are at once a dishonor to those who constantly repeat them, and an intolerable nuisance to those whose ears are jaded with them."[72]

Paul ends his list of various parts of spiritual armor by identifying the one offensive weapon we have been given for the fight, namely "the sword of the Spirit, which is the word of God."[73] Even though the sword completes the list, Paul finishes the sentence by adding, "praying at all times in the Spirit, with all prayer and

---

[72]C. H. Spurgeon. *Lectures to My Students: Complete & Unabridged. Ministry Resources Library.* (Grand Rapids, Mich.: Zondervan Publishing House, 1989), 63.
[73]Ephesians 6:17

supplication."[74] And he continues the thought: "To that end, keep alert with all perseverance, making supplication for all the saints, and also for me, that words may be given to me in opening my mouth boldly to proclaim the mystery of the gospel, for which I am an ambassador in chains, that I may declare it boldly, as I ought to speak."[75]

We have been given a mighty sword with which to fight. Whether we consider prayer a powerful strategy or another weapon for the battle, the combination of the Word of God with prayer is a powerful force for advancing the glorious purposes of our King, for whom we are all ambassadors. May God grant us every grace we need to be alert with all perseverance and boldness in prayer and supplication so that the next generation might know the mystery of the Gospel, "the children yet unborn, and arise and tell them to their children, so that they should set their hope in God."[76]

> **"Whether we consider prayer a powerful strategy or another weapon for the battle, the combination of the Word of God with prayer is a powerful force for advancing the glorious purposes of our King, for whom we are all ambassadors."**
>
> —DAVID MICHAEL

[74]Ephesians 6:18
[75]Ephesians 6:18-20
[76]Psalm 78:6-7

Prayers for the Next Generation

Both churches that I have served over the past three decades provide parents an opportunity to stand before the congregation with their children, make five solemn promises, and dedicate their children to the Lord. The service concludes with a pastoral prayer of dedication that expresses our gratitude to God for these children and our hope that they will belong wholly to God, through Jesus Christ, forever. I am trusting that the Lord has been pleased to answer these prayers for hundreds of parents and children who have participated.

Below are a few of the dedication prayers from these services. I hope they will serve as examples of big, bold, biblical pleas for the sake of the next generation, and expressions of gratitude to the One who gives and sustains the lives and faith of our children.

I am including these sample prayers because I know how much I appreciated having a book of Spurgeon's pulpit prayers to stir my own heart for prayer and to influence the way I was praying. My hope is that these sample prayers will stimulate an outpouring of big, bold, biblical prayers for the next generation from the hearts of God's people. Remember that the words of these prayers are expressing the heart of a pastor at a moment in time in a congregation with a specific group of parents and children in mind.

The words of our prayers matter, but the heart behind the words matters more. The substance of these prayers came from reading and reflecting on God's Word. Often, I would come to a passage that struck a responsive chord in my heart that prompted a spontaneous prayer like, "Yes Lord, that's what I want for my children!" I simply took that desire inspired by God's Word and turned it into a prayer.

Taking the time to get in touch with what I desire for my children, letting the Truth and promises of God shape and inform those desires, and then investing the time to find words to express those desires has been very fruitful. It is what God has used for decades to sustain a passion to pursue a vision for the next generation that is dependent on Him "to do far more abundantly than all that we ask or think"[77] in our big, bold, biblical prayers.

Well Done, Good and Faithful Servant!

O God, our Father,

Once again, You have placed before us a magnificent display of Your glory. These children, who once did not exist except in the mind of their Creator, are now living, breathing, thinking, moving, growing human beings who will exist forever. We bless You, Father, and praise You for giving these children to their parents, and for adding them to this congregation.

When You gave us these children, You gave us a wonderful gift. You have given us the opportunity to invest our lives in something that is eternal. You have given us the joy of seeing the world through their eyes, and watching them grow into mature men and women. You have given us more people to love, care for, and share life with. There are hundreds of earthly reasons to rejoice in these children; but Lord, there is a greater joy—a higher one that we desire. We want to see these children praise Your name. We want the Holy Spirit to ignite a flame of passion

> "Taking the time to get in touch with what I desire for my children, letting the truth and promises of God shape and inform those desires, and then investing the time to find words to express those desires has been very fruitful."
>
> —DAVID MICHAEL

---
[77] Ephesians 3:20

for You in their souls that rises in rapturous love and mighty adoration. We want their tongues to declare a conviction, rising from the depths of their souls that the Lord lives, and blessed be my rock, let the God of my salvation be exalted. He is my God, and I will extol Him. He is my father's God and I will prepare Him a habitation.

So, Lord, let these children praise You. Incline their hearts toward You and toward Your Word. Open the eyes of their hearts so they can see wonderful things from Your Word. Enlighten their hearts so they can see Your glory in everything. Give each of them a heart united in affection for You so they might fear Your name and walk in the Truth. Help them to look to You for satisfaction and not to the world. According to the riches of Your glory, strengthen these children with power through Your Spirit. And give them a joy so strong and full that it spreads and expands for the joy of others. And may their lives abound with good deeds so the glory of God might be seen in their lives.

Lord, hear this prayer for each one of these children. Forbid that one of these be lost to the world. We want each one to run their race and finish well.

O God, help us! Help us to be all that You have called us to be for these children. I pray that these parents would be examples to their children of the kind of people we pray they will become. Keep them strong in the Lord and in the power of Your might. Keep them walking close to You. Keep their eyes fixed on what is eternal. Give them wisdom, discernment, patience, endurance, courage, faith, and all the other gifts and graces they need to do what they cannot do apart from You. In their weakness, magnify the perfection of Your power.

And, Lord, I pray that we as a congregation would be faithful to the promises we have made to You and to these parents today. Keep us faithful in teaching, preaching, and living the Word of God before them. Keep us faithful in our efforts to encourage and support these parents. Keep us faithful until the end. And when we see You face to face, may it be said of these children and these parents and this congregation, "Well done, good and faithful [servants]. You have been faithful...Enter into the joy of your master."[78]

We ask these things in Jesus' name. Amen!

Reigning with Christ in Everlasting Joy

Almighty God,

We thank You for the gift of these children, and for these parents who recognize that from You and through You and to You are all things, including these children.

You already know these children better than any of us do, and that will always be so. Though hidden from us, they have not been hidden from You since they were first conceived in Your mind.

Your eyes saw them at conception. You created the very core of their beings. You knit them together in their mothers' wombs. You ordained their last breath, even before they took their first. You know the very second they fall asleep and the instant they wake. You know every thought they think, every move they make, and every detail of their lives today, tomorrow, and for the months and years to come.

Before a sound, word, or cry ever vibrates their vocal cords, You know it completely. Lord, it is our earnest prayer that those vocal cords vibrate praise to You from hearts that overflow with affection for You.

We pray that these children be given everything they need to serve You faithfully and fruitfully all of their days. We ask that they would come to know the fear of the Lord, and spend their days hungering for You, trusting in You, and consumed with a passion for You.

We ask You, dear Father, that Your Word would dwell richly in their hearts, as well as in their heads. Let it season their speech

[78]Matthew 25:21

and influence every dimension of their lives. Give them lives that are excellent in conduct, and give them character that has the aroma of Christ. Give them thoughts that are true, honorable, right, pure, lovely, and of good repute. Please give them children and grandchildren and great grandchildren who are blessed of God, mighty in faith, and fervent in prayer.

And, Lord Jesus Christ, on that day when night shall be no more, let them see Your face and reign with You in joy forever and ever. Give these parents and this congregation everything we need to be faithful to the calling that is upon us for Jesus' sake, and for the exultation of His name, and for the joy of the generations to come, we pray. Amen!

500 Trillion Years from Now

Dear Father,

We join these parents in giving heartfelt thanks to You for the gift of these children. Out of nothing, You have brought this moment and these children into being. With a mighty, sovereign hand, You have sustained every breath and every heartbeat and everything else that keeps these children and all the rest of us alive and growing. We ask, LORD, that You will keep sustaining and protecting so that 70, 80, 100 years from now, each of these children could look back on a long, productive, and fruitful life.

Even more LORD, we ask that You accomplish for these children all that needs to happen in their lives so that 500 trillion years from now they are in the shelter of the Most High—resting in the shadow of the Almighty, and looking ahead to an eternity of joy and satisfaction in You.

Make these next decades of their lives count for eternity. Claim them as Your children, LORD! Early in life, set their minds to study Your Word. Show them Your salvation, and lead them to a knowledge of the Truth. Give them a pure heart, a good conscience, and a sincere faith. Fill their lives with godliness and dignity. Make them fighters, LORD—fighters in the fight of faith. Even if a thousand fall at their side and 10,000 at their right hands, keep their eyes fixed on You. Keep them well clothed in spiritual armor. Be their Shield and Fortress. Keep the enemy's weapons from penetrating their souls.

Make these years count for the Kingdom, too. Make these children instruments of revival in the 21st century. So shine on them that they may reflect Your glory to the world. So dwell in them that Your power flows out of their lives to work miracles in their generation. Through these children, give their generation gifted teachers of the Word and bold witnesses to the power of Christ.

No one can deny the impact these parents will have on their children, for better or for worse. Oh God, give them everything they need to make it for the better. Help them to be what You have called them to be as parents. May these children grow up in functional homes. Fill these parents with Your Spirit. Anoint them with power for this calling that You have placed upon their lives. Give them discernment and wisdom for every situation. Make them examples of godly manhood and womanhood in the home and the world.

LORD, You have sworn, by Yourself, and by Your own name, that You will bear us up as on eagle's wings. As parents, and as a congregation entrusted with these children, we cast ourselves on You and ask that You lead these children, and that You lead us. Lead us into perfect holiness. Lead us to glory. Lead us to the Kingdom that is yet to come so that 500 trillion years and beyond we will still be declaring, as we do now, glory to the Father, glory to the Son, glory to the Holy Spirit, and as saints triumphant through all the ages long, we will still be singing that eternal song, *May Jesus Christ be Praised.*

In that great name, we pray. Amen!

Run with Endurance

O Lord,

We thank You for these parents and for putting in their hearts the desire to raise these children in the discipline and instruction of the Lord, and to seek Your help in building the Word of God, the character of Christ, and the joy of the Lord into their lives. We ask that, according to Your grace, You would help them keep the promises they have made and establish the desire of their hearts with power in order that the name of our Lord Jesus may be glorified in them and in their children. O Lord, we pray that they will be well supplied for the challenges that lie ahead. May they find the faith, strength, wisdom, patience, understanding, courage, and all the other graces they need for a job that is impossible apart from You.

Lord, we earnestly pray that these children will be among those who love Christ and keep His commands. Subdue every impulse for evil. Bring every thought captive to the obedience of Christ, and conform them to the image of Your Son. We don't ask that they be spared pain or sorrow, but that they run with endurance the race set before them. Let them grow in grace and in the likeness of our Savior, so You can look upon them as sons and daughters in Christ and see with delight the work of Your own hands.

And Lord, we pray that the Spirit of God would rest like a cloud over this congregation and upon this people who care about these children and the outcome of their faith. May these children see in us the evidence of hearts inflamed with a passion for God. May they witness an intense desire for the increase of Your Kingdom, for the preservation of Your Truth, and for the display of that Truth to the world in all its sanctifying power.

May we be examples of the kind of people we long for them to become—with clear insight into Your Word, living in close fellowship with You, growing in the likeness of Your character, and in zeal for Your glory, and may we be a people who will one day, by Your grace, look into Your smiling face and enjoy You forever. O Lord, hear the prayer of our hearts. In Jesus' name, we pray. Amen!

Who, Except You?

What God is there like our God?

Who except You, dear Father, could weave these children together and sustain their lives and the lives of their parents to this moment? Who except You could have orchestrated the endless number of choices and decisions that were made generations ago to place these children in the arms of these parents, in this church, surrounded by this congregation, on this day, in this moment of history? Surely, this simple scene before us is a showcase of Your glory, which declares the mighty and creative work of Your hands!

Now Father, according to Your sovereign and loving purpose established long ago, we ask that Your mighty hand continue this great work! Don't let these parents forget the calling on their lives or forsake the responsibilities that You have given them. Give them increasing affections for You, which are authentic and contagious to these children. Give them wisdom to respond to every parental challenge in a way that directs their children far from destruction and onto a path that leads to life.

We also ask that You keep us faithful as a congregation to our covenant promises and to the commitment we have made to these parents. May this church always be a place where these parents are loved, challenged, encouraged, supported, and helped. May these children, and their children and their children's children grow up in a church that genuinely cares about the outcome of their faith and remains radically committed to a God-centered, Christ-exalting vision for them, for this city, and for the world. Give them many people in this congregation who will pray for them and join their parents in making Your glory known to them.

And Lord, we ask that You do what we can't do. We ask that You call each of these children to Yourself. Please Father, give them hearts that trust in Jesus and desire to walk in all Your ways. Fill their mouths with Your praises, and let their souls boast in You. Give them a life-giving fear of You, and don't let them ever exchange the Truth of God for a lie, nor serve the created rather than the Creator of all things. We pray that You will give them an unshakable faith and a life that is fruitfully invested for Your glory. Keep them persevering until they take their last breath, and then gather them together with all Your people from every tribe and tongue and nation to worship before the throne. And let them exalt Your name and enjoy You forever. Amen!

Hope in What Is Certain

Almighty God,

As we look at these babies that are before us, we can imagine what their lives will be like. We can hope for what they will become. These parents can teach and nurture and guide and direct these children toward that hope, but we are aware—sometimes all too painfully aware—just how tentative our hopes and dreams for our children can be. We fully expect for there to be twists and turns in the lives of these children that none of us are prepared for, or can even imagine right now, which is why we come to You this morning.

We come to You because You are God, and there is no other. We come to you because You are God, and there is none like You. You are the One who declares "the end from the beginning." You are the One who has declared "from ancient times things not yet done." You are the One who says, "My counsel shall stand, and I will accomplish all my purpose."[79]

So, Lord, together with these parents, we lift these children to You, and stand confidentlyl in the face of uncertainty because of what is irrefutably certain. We are certain that these children have been created for Your glory. We are certain that, if they call

[79]Isaiah 46:9-10

on the name of the Lord, they will be saved. We plead that they will, so that "neither death nor life, nor angels nor rulers, nor things present nor things to come, nor powers, nor height nor depth, nor anything else in all creation, will be able to separate [them] from the love of God in Christ Jesus our Lord."[80] We are certain that You cause all things to work together for good for those who love You, to those who are called according to Your purpose.

So Lord, more than wealth or fame, more than a good education, a good job, a nice home, and a strong family, more than health, more than friends and a good spouse someday, more than a long and fruitful life, we pray with all of our hearts that each of these children will be born again. We pray that they will be called according to Your purpose. We pray that You will open their eyes to see their need, and give them the will and the power to call upon the name of the Lord as their God. Lord, we surrender all worldly claim. Take everything from them, if You must, but give them Jesus, in whose great name we pray. Amen!

You Are the Reason

Almighty God,

We bow before You as the Creator, the Giver, the Sustainer, and the Taker of all life.

There would be no reason to stand here this morning were it not for the fact that a holy God worked wonders with perfect faithfulness, according to plans formed long ago. You are the reason there is a dedication service! You are the God of these parents, and of these children, and of all who are assembled here. We exalt You! We give thanks to Your name, and we commend these children to You in the hope that they will do the same.

O God, You have established Your name, and You will make it known in every generation. We pray Father, that all these children will believe in You and will be faithful in making Your

---

[80]Romans 8:38-39

name known to their children. Let it be that their children would declare the glories of Your name to their children, and to their children's children. One thing we ask Father, this is what we seek for these children, that they may dwell in the house of the Lord all the days of their lives, and that their eyes may see the beauty of the Lord and seek You with all their hearts.

So please, Father, direct their hearts to You. Plant in them the desire to do Your will—a desire that exceeds all other desires. Set their hearts and minds on things that are above, and not on earthly things. To that end, we ask that You will guard the hearts and minds of these parents and this congregation in Christ Jesus. May we spend our lives before these children on things that are excellent and worthy of praise. May our thoughts and activities be devoted to what is true, noble, right, pure, lovely, and admirable.

We ask that You would instruct these parents in the way they should go as they seek to fulfill the promises they have just made. Help them to faithfully instruct their children, and teach them the way that leads to life. Counsel them through all the difficulties and perplexities of parenting. Watch over them. Sustain their trust and their confidence in You. May their duties to each other and to their children be their delight and their joy.

And Lord, I pray for each of us who added our "Amen!" to the words of dedication. Help us to keep our promise to assist these parents with the education of their children in the Christian faith. Breathe on every Sunday school worker, every nursery worker, every youth leader, and every parent to the end that these children may be ignited with a passion for You. Help us to equip them well to take Your Word and the hope of the Gospel from this place to this city and to other cities, to this land and to other lands, to this people and to other peoples until the nations come and honor the One who surrendered Himself to the cross.

And Lord, I pray that these children will one day join us in taking a stand against the rising spirit of indifference, alienation, and hostility in our land toward various races and toward the unborn.

Let them grow to become bold in speech and courageous in action, and may walls and structures that support abortion and racism in this land crumble one day before their eyes.

Apart from You, Lord Jesus, the hope and vision of this prayer is nothing. Our faith looks to You and You alone to do what we cannot do, and to accomplish more than we ask or imagine. Magnify Your name in the lives of these children. Magnify Your name in these families. Magnify Your name among the people of this church. We ask it all in the mighty name of Jesus. Amen!

Blessed Be the Lord our God

Blessed be the Lord our God, who has made heaven and earth, who spoke each of these children into being, and who has not forsaken His loving kindness to them or their parents.

Blessed be the great Searcher and Knower of all—who knows when [Lincoln] sits, and when [Matthew] rises, and who perceives [Sylvia]'s thoughts from afar.

Blessed be the One who discerns [Joshua]'s going out and his lying down, and who is—and always will be—familiar with all of [Isabel]'s ways.

Blessed be the One who already knows the first, as well as the last word that will be on [Jonathan]'s tongue.

Blessed be the One who hemmed [Josiah] in—before and behind—and who laid His mighty hand on [Grace Elizabeth].

Blessed be the Lord, who will daily bear each burden and will be attentive to the prayers of these parents and their children.

Blessed be the rock of our salvation, and the Father of our Lord Jesus Christ, to whom we look for mercy in the hope that each of these children will be born again to a living hope, and will obtain an inheritance, which is imperishable and undefiled and will not fade away.

Dear Father, as we acknowledge these children as gifts from You, we are trusting in You, and Your unchanging nature and unbreakable promises. We believe that You, the God who was with Adam in the garden, with Moses in Egypt, with Abraham in Beersheba, with David in Hebron and Elijah at Mt. Carmel, with Peter and John on their way to the temple, and with Saul on his way to Damascus will be with these children and their parents wherever You lead them.

We commend them to You in the sure and certain hope that You are righteous in all Your ways and kind in all Your deeds. These promises are impossible to keep apart from You, and yet we make them boldly with confidence that You will be near to these parents, and conform their desires for their children to Yours.

We believe that You will establish these children firm in faith so that their eyes will look to You for all they need, and their mouths will speak the praise of the Lord and bless Your holy name forever.

May these children never be without examples of godly men and women of faith who are willing to invest in their lives and can help us keep the promises we as a congregation have made to You and to these parents.

Finally, Lord, keep us faithful until the end when we see You face to face and when, by Your grace, these parents and this congregation enter into the joy of the One whose glorious name is blessed forever. Amen!

We Ask for More!

Almighty God,

We praise You and bless the day that You spoke these children into being, gave them the breath of life, and now have sustained them to this moment. This is no small thing You have done. This is no insignificant blessing. But Lord, with all humility, and with all the confidence that we have in Christ Jesus, we ask for more.

We ask that they will die to the sin nature that they have inherited as sons and daughters of Adam. Instead of being children of wrath, dead in their trespasses and sins, we ask that You raise them up to new life in Christ Jesus.

In Jesus' name, we ask that You lead them out of darkness and into Your glorious light. We ask that You rescue them from the kingdom of Satan and make them citizens of Your unshakable Kingdom. Let them be poor in this world, if they must, but make them rich in faith and heirs of the Kingdom that You have promised to all that love You.

We want them to desire You more than anything else because You are infinitely more than anything else that they need. There is no limit to Your goodness. Your riches are unsearchable. You have every good thing within Your reach, and Your supply never runs out. O God, be their portion forever. Draw them close to Yourself, and hold them secure with the cords of Your love.

May there be for these children no rivals to Your throne. May they have no other god but God Almighty. May they have no treasure but Jesus Christ their Savior. Let no spirit's power have any dominion over them except the power of Your Holy Spirit working righteousness and peace within them. Capture every thought, every desire, every dream, every word, and every act. And let them be under Your glory and sovereign purposes in their lives. Let them live and move and have their being in You.

Reign in their lives. May every body, soul, and spirit be dedicated completely to You. Sit on the throne of every life. Rule them, and may the life they live prove that they follow Jesus Christ alone as their Lord.

Use them to flood this land with streams of righteousness. Shine on them so they can reflect Your light to this fallen world. Dwell in them so that out of them will come the power of Your life to influence the world. May those who laugh and sneer at them and say that the Gospel has lost its power be made foolish by the wisdom of the Most High God at work in and through them.

And Lord, together with these parents and this people who care about the faith of these children, I ask that we will have all the grace that is needed to love these children and inspire them to fear You, to walk in all Your ways, and to delight in You both now and forever. Amen!

Truth78 Inauguration Prayer for the Next Generation

On April 10, 2018 we gathered in Louisville to celebrate 20 years of God's faithfulness through the ministry of Children Desiring God. With hearts that were full and a task before us that was great, we lifted up the following prayer to our King as we were commissioned under our new name, Truth78.

Almighty God,

We bow before You with grateful hearts that You have made known to us Your glorious deeds and Your might and the wonders You have done. We will forever give thanks for those You inspired to record Your words in a book. We thank You for those with steadfast hearts and faithful spirits who taught us from Your Word the Truth about what we once were and what we have become in Christ Jesus.

- Once lost—now found.

- Once far off—now brought near.

- Once alienated from the commonwealth of Israel—now fellow citizens with the saints.

- Once we were not a people—now we are a people.

- Once slaves to sin—now children of God.

- Once dead in trespasses and sins—now alive with Christ.

- Once enemies—now seated at Your table.

- Once children of wrath—now the redeemed of the Lord.

- Once enslaved to sinful passions—now set free for good works.

- Once sons of disobedience—now fellow heirs with Christ.

- Once bearing fruit for death—now reaping eternal life.

- Once separated from Christ—now seated with Him in the heavenly places.

- Once without hope—now heirs of immeasurable riches of grace.

- Once condemned—now without condemnation.

- Once bound by the law of sin and death—now set free by the law of the Spirit of life.

- Once following the prince of the power of the air—now led by the Ancient of Days.

Lord, I pray that the Truth that has been entrusted to us and the lessons we have learned will not be hidden from the next generation. Grant us every grace to make known to our children, even the children yet unborn, the path that leads to life. Make us a generation of parents, educators, pastors, resource developers, publishers, writers, translators, supporters, and partners who will teach them Your ways and how to walk according to the Truth so that they might set their hope and confidence in You, and not forget Your works.

Give to our children, and to their children, souls anchored in heaven. Sustain in them a deep and substantial assurance of things hoped for, like Abel and Enoch and Noah and Abraham and Isaac and Moses and Gideon and Barak and Samson and Jephthah and David and Samuel and the prophets and all the saints who, through faith, obtained the promise.

Turn the hearts of the next generations away from the deceptive promises of sin and toward the all-satisfying promises of God, who swears by Himself, that they might be strong, confident, secure, ready, and bold to lay down their lives for the sake of the ministry and the glory of God.

May our children live as sojourners in this world, who desire You and all that You have promised more than they desire money, more than power, more than popularity, more than anything else. Give them faith to be strong and faith to be weak, faith to be married and faith to be single, faith to have children and faith to be childless, faith to be wealthy and faith to be poor. Give them faith that can stand even when crisis comes and when tragedy strikes.

May they never lose sight of the reality that You are better than what life can give them now, and better than what death can take from them later. Give them faith to suffer willingly as they await something better than what this earth can offer. May their hunger for the superior worth of our glorious God be so great that bridges are burned to a hundred sins and a hundred fears.

May they yield to You as a Father who disciplines those He loves, and who comes to us painfully and mysteriously through the hostility of sinful adversaries and the natural disasters of a fallen world. Make them submissive to Your sovereign, fatherly care, and may they not grow weary or lose heart.

Help them lay aside every encumbrance and the sin that so easily entangles, so they can run the race You have set before them, holding fast to hope and holding firm their confidence until that day when Your Kingdom comes in all its glory, and Truth once and for all triumphs over sin and death and mourning and tears and all that hinders the everlasting joy that is ours through Jesus Christ. Amen!

"Give ear, O my people, to my teaching; incline your ears to the words of my mouth! ²I will open my mouth in a parable; I will utter dark sayings from of old, ³things that we have heard and known, that our fathers have told us. ⁴We will not hide them from their children, but tell to the coming generation the glorious deeds of the LORD, and his might, and the wonders that he has done. ⁵He established a testimony in Jacob and appointed a law in Israel, which he commanded our fathers to teach to their children, ⁶that the next generation might know them, the children yet unborn, and arise and tell them to their children, ⁷so that they should set their hope in God and not forget the works of God, but keep his commandments; ⁸and that they should not be like their fathers, a stubborn and rebellious generation, a generation whose heart was not steadfast, whose spirit was not faithful to God."

—PSALM 78:1-8

A Mother's and Grandmother's Prayers for the Next Generation— by Sally Michael

1,110 miles. That's the distance between me and my grandchildren. How does a grandmother influence her grandchildren with such distance between them? There are no daily interactions, no regular opportunities to sit down with the Word of God to instruct them, no impromptu "seize the real-life moment" conversations to apply spiritual Truth. But God is not limited by space and time...and His Word is powerful. I may not be able to have a regular physical presence in my grandchildren's lives, but I can have a regular spiritual influence through prayer.

When I consider these words from 19th-century British Pastor John Angell James, I am inspired to pray earnestly for eternal things for my children and grandchildren:

> My subject is religion—my object is the soul—my aim is
> salvation...I look beyond the painted and gaudy scene of
> earth's fading vanities, to the everlasting ages through which
> you must exist in torment or bliss; and, God helping me,
> it shall not be my fault if you do not live in comfort, die in
> peace, and inherit salvation![81]

How do I look beyond the immediate temporary things, "the gaudy scene of earth's fading vanities" to pray the weighty and eternal matters of the soul? In my experience, turning to the Word of God helps me focus my mind and heart, lifts me above this world, and sets my mind "on things that are above."[82] I find

---

[81] John Angell James. *Female Piety: or, The Young Woman's Friend and Guide through Life to Immortality.* Edited by Don Kistler. (Orlando, Fla.: Soli Deo Gloria Publishing, 1999), 2.
[82] Colossians 3:2

no better way to pray "big," weighty prayers for my children and grandchildren than with an open Bible before me. It is there that I find God's thoughts and words to pray for the next generation.

Almost any portion of Scripture can inspire prayer for the next generation—whether it be a Bible story, a psalm, a proverb, a Gospel passage, or the letters of the Apostles. Focusing on the truths of a passage and considering how these truths relate to the lives of my children and grandchildren helps me turn a passage of Scripture into a prayer of praise, an expression of gratitude, a confession or petition that fuels passionate prayer. I offer the following prayers for my grandchildren as examples of Bible-saturated prayers for the next generation.

A Prayer for Our Grandson, Joshua, Inspired by 1 Samuel 17

God delivers Goliath into the hands of Israel through David.

Lord, may You be praised as the God of all the earth. You are the LORD of hosts who delivers Your people. May Joshua know that You alone are God, that You are greater than any enemy, any problem, any situation he faces. Give him a faith like David to see You as all-sufficient, almighty, and faithful. Help him face the obstacles in his life, knowing that You have been faithful in the past, and You will be faithful in the future. Give him the confidence that with him stands a God who will battle for him, a God who cannot be defeated, the living God who is an ever-present help in time of trouble. May his confidence be in You, and not in himself. Give him a zeal for Your great name so that he will be a fearless witness of Your greatness and stand against those who would defy Your name. Amen.

A Prayer for Our Granddaughter, Anna, Inspired by Psalm 16:11

You make known to me the path of life; in your presence there is fullness of joy; at your right hand are pleasures forevermore.

Almighty God, in You there is fullness of joy. You are the God who gives eternal pleasure, outweighing the temporary, anemic pleasures of this world. Make known to Anna the path of life. Give her eyes to see that this world has nothing to offer, and that You are the Way, the Truth, and the Life. Lead her into sure and secure saving faith—a faith that is unshakable, and an inheritance that is imperishable. Give her a joy in Your presence and a love for Your Word that gives life. Open her eyes to Your glory, and fill her soul with the joy only found in knowing You, trusting You, and living in fellowship with You. Enlighten her mind to understand that the pleasures of this world are fleeting and empty. Do not let her put her confidence in broken cisterns, but capture her heart to trust You, devote herself to You above all else, and discover her greatest pleasure in pleasing You. Help her to seek those things that are above and not on the earth. May she experience eternal pleasure at Your right hand in this life, and then forever and ever in Your presence. Amen.

A Prayer for Our Grandson, Joshua, with Wording from Psalm 119

Dear God, may Joshua know the blessing of those who keep Your testimonies, and may he seek You with his whole heart. Help him to keep his way pure by guarding it according to Your Word. Help him store up Your Word in his heart so that he might not sin against You. Open his eyes, that he may behold wondrous things out of Your Law. Make Your testimonies his delight and his counselors. Enlarge his heart that he will run in the way of Your commandments. Give him understanding, that he may keep Your Law and observe it with his whole heart. Incline his heart to Your testimonies, and not to selfish gain! Turn his eyes from looking at worthless things; and give him life in Your ways. Amen.

A Prayer for Our Granddaughter, Katie, Inspired by Proverbs 3:5-7

Trust in the LORD with all your heart, and do not lean on your own understanding. ⁶In all your ways acknowledge him, and he will make straight your paths. ⁷Be not wise in your own eyes; fear the LORD, and turn away from evil.

O God, I praise You because You are trustworthy, all-knowing, and all-wise. You are good, and in You there is no darkness. Thank You for Your promises, which are tried and true. Thank You for Your Word, which guides, enlightens, protects, and comforts. I pray, dear Lord, that Katie will trust in You with all her heart—that she will put her full confidence in You, that she will know that You are her Creator and the Ruler of heaven and earth, and that You are all-loving, all-powerful, and all-wise. Help her not to lean on her own understanding, but to evaluate everything according to Your Word. Help her to look to You for guidance, and to know that Truth is found in Your Word. I pray that she would seek You each day, look to You when making decisions, lean on You for daily strength, and put Your glory as her highest desire. Lead her and make her paths straight. Do not let her wander to the left or to the right, but keep her trusting You and Your commands without wavering. Keep her from pride and give her a humble dependence on You. Bless her with a godly fear of You—a fear of offending You, of walking away from You, of ignoring Your counsel, of being outside of fellowship with You. Give her resolve and strength to turn away from evil...and to turn to You that she might praise Your great name forever, and bring glory to You. Amen.

A Prayer for Our Daughter, Kristi, Inspired by Jeremiah 17:7-8

"Blessed is the man who trusts in the LORD, whose trust is the LORD. ⁸He is like a tree planted by water, that sends out its roots by the stream, and does not fear when heat comes, for its leaves remain green, and is not anxious in the year of drought, for it does not cease to bear fruit."

> "Like a tree planted by water, may she sink her roots deeply into Your Word, so that she is grounded securely with confidence in Your promises, holding fast to her salvation..."
>
> —SALLY MICHAEL

Dear God, I praise You that Your name is Yahweh, the self-existent, sovereign, almighty, eternal, unchanging God. Sustain in Kristi an unshakable trust in who You are, a faith that trusts Your sovereign plan for her life, and an enduring satisfaction in Your steadfast love in every season of her life. Whether in times of abundance and joy, or times of trial and suffering, may she rest secure in Your unchanging love and faithfulness. Like a tree planted by water, may she sink her roots deeply into Your Word, so that she is grounded securely with confidence in Your promises, holding fast to her salvation and crowned with the beautiful green canopy of faith so that others may see Your life-giving grace in her. Give her the grace to face the future with the confident assurance of Your presence, Your strength, and Your peace, through whatever Your sovereign will ordains for her. Bring her through the fire and water of whatever trials may come, to a place of abundance. Give her the faith to fight the fiery darts of anxiety and fear with the steadfast confidence that You will never leave her or forsake her. May Kingdom fruit abound in every season of her life to the praise of Your glorious name. Amen.

A Prayer for Our Daughter, Amy, Inspired by John 15:4-5

"Abide in me, and I in you. As the branch cannot bear fruit by itself, unless it abides in the vine, neither can you, unless you abide in me. ⁵I am the vine; you are the branches. Whoever abides in me and I in him, he it is that bears much fruit, for apart from me you can do nothing."

Jesus, I praise You as the Vine, the all-sufficient, eternal, and inexhaustible Source of life and strength for Your people. I praise You for all You have done to secure my daughter to You, the eternal life-giving Vine. I pray that Amy will continue to abide in You and never boast or depend on her own gifts and abilities and determination. Give her the grace to trust You daily and lean on You fully, and to humbly and consistently depend on You for all that she needs. Keep her abiding in You so that she bears much fruit, not from herself but through Your power that is at work in her. May she draw her strength from walking in close fellowship with You, her wisdom from the Truth of Your Word, and her joy from seeking You. Cause her to flourish as a strong branch, drawing its sustenance from life-giving dependence on You. May she be fruitful in her roles as a wife, mother, church member, and witness to a dying world until that day when she will abide in the joy of Your presence forever and ever. Amen.

A Prayer for Our Son-in-Law, Gary, Inspired by 2 Corinthians 5:20

Therefore, we are ambassadors for Christ, God making his appeal through us. We implore you on behalf of Christ, be reconciled to God.

Dear God, what an unspeakable honor it is that You have made Your children to be Your ambassadors and have given my son-in-law the privilege of representing You as a teacher in a place of influence with students, teachers, and leaders. For all his days, may he be a faithful representative of the name he bears as a follower of Jesus Christ. May he never shrink from speaking the Truth with boldness and courage. Make him an example to his students of a faithful ambassador of the Truth. Give him the wisdom and discernment to know what Truth his students need to hear, when they need to hear it, and how best to deliver it with grace and wisdom. Give him the love of Christ for those who whose hearts are drawn away from Christ and who are tempted to walk according to the foolishness of the world. May Gary's life and words to be a testimony of the beauty of knowing You. Give him opportunity to implore his students to be reconciled to You. Make him a faithful witness, pastor, and shepherd to this flock You have entrusted to him. Help him to see their spiritual need as greater than their academic need, and cause him to be a faithful testimony of Your grace for the glory of Christ and the everlasting joy of all who are influenced by Gary through Christ, in whose name I pray. Amen.

More Bible Passages to Pray for the Next Generation

Oh, taste and see that the LORD is good! Blessed is the man who takes refuge in him! (Psalm 34:8)

"I delight to do your will, O my God; your law is within my heart." (Psalm 40:8)

When I am afraid, I put my trust in you. ⁴In God, whose word I praise, in God I trust; I shall not be afraid. What can flesh do to me? (Psalm 56:3-4)

Teach me your way, O LORD, that I may walk in your truth; unite my heart to fear your name. (Psalm 86:11)

Those who trust in the LORD are like Mount Zion, which cannot be moved, but abides forever. ²As the mountains surround Jerusalem, so the LORD surrounds his people, from this time forth and forevermore. (Psalm 125:1-2)

My son, do not despise the LORD's discipline or be weary of his reproof, ¹²for the LORD reproves him whom he loves, as a father the son in whom he delights. (Proverbs 3:11-12)

My son, keep your father's commandment, and forsake not your mother's teaching. ²¹Bind them on your heart always; tie them around your neck. ²²When you walk, they will lead you; when you lie down, they will watch over you; and when you awake, they will talk with you. ²³For the commandment is a lamp and the teaching a light, and the reproofs of discipline are the way of life, (Proverbs 6:20-23)

Listen to advice and accept instruction, that you may gain wisdom in the future. (Proverbs 19:20)

"Seek the LORD while he may be found; call upon him while he is near; ⁷let the wicked forsake his way, and the unrighteous man his thoughts; let him return to the LORD, that he may have compassion on him, and to our God, for he will abundantly pardon." (Isaiah 55:6-7)

"Blessed are the poor in spirit, for theirs is the kingdom of heaven. ⁴Blessed are those who mourn, for they shall be comforted. ⁵Blessed are the meek, for they shall inherit the earth. ⁶Blessed are those who hunger and thirst for righteousness, for they shall be satisfied. ⁷Blessed are the merciful, for they shall receive mercy. ⁸Blessed are the pure in heart, for they shall see God. ⁹Blessed are the peacemakers, for they shall be called sons of God. ¹⁰Blessed are those who are persecuted for righteousness' sake, for theirs is the kingdom of heaven. ¹¹Blessed are you when others revile you and persecute you and utter all kinds of evil against you falsely on my account. ¹²Rejoice and be glad, for your reward is great in heaven, for so they persecuted the prophets who were before you." (Matthew 5:3-12)

"Do not lay up for yourselves treasures on earth, where moth and rust destroy and where thieves break in and steal, ²⁰but lay up for yourselves treasures in heaven, where neither moth nor rust destroys and where thieves do not break in and steal. ²¹For where your treasure is, there your heart will be also." (Matthew 6:19-21)

But to all who did receive him, who believed in his name, he gave the right to become children of God, ¹³who were born, not of blood nor of the will of the flesh nor of the will of man, but of God. (John 1:12-13)

For this light momentary affliction is preparing for us an eternal weight of glory beyond all comparison, ¹⁸as we look not to the things that are seen but to the things that are unseen. For the things that are seen are transient, but the things that are unseen are eternal. (2 Corinthians 4:17-18)

Be angry and do not sin; do not let the sun go down on your anger, ²⁷and give no opportunity to the devil. (Ephesians 4:26-27)

Let all bitterness and wrath and anger and clamor and slander be put away from you, along with all malice. ³²Be kind to one another, tenderhearted, forgiving one another, as God in Christ forgave you. (Ephesians 4:31-32)

Therefore be imitators of God, as beloved children. ²And walk in love, as Christ loved us and gave himself up for us, a fragrant offering and sacrifice to God. (Ephesians 5:1-2)

Finally, be strong in the Lord and in the strength of his might. ¹¹Put on the whole armor of God, that you may be able to stand against the schemes of the devil. (Ephesians 6:10-11)

Finally, brothers, whatever is true, whatever is honorable, whatever is just, whatever is pure, whatever is lovely, whatever is commendable, if there is any excellence, if there is anything worthy of praise, think about these things. ⁹What you have learned and received and heard and seen in me— practice these things, and the God of peace will be with you. (Philippians 4:8-9)

And so, from the day we heard, we have not ceased to pray for you, asking that you may be filled with the knowledge of his will in all spiritual wisdom and understanding, ¹⁰so as to walk in a manner worthy of the Lord, fully pleasing to him: bearing fruit in every good work and increasing in the knowledge of God; ¹¹being strengthened with all power, according to his glorious might, for all endurance and patience with joy; ¹²giving thanks to the Father, who has qualified you to share in the inheritance of the saints in light. (Colossians 1:9-12)

If then you have been raised with Christ, seek the things that are above, where Christ is, seated at the right hand of God. ²Set your minds on things that are above, not on things that are on earth. ³For you have died, and your life is hidden with Christ in God. (Colossians 3:1-3)

And we urge you, brothers, admonish the idle, encourage the fainthearted, help the weak, be patient with them all. ¹⁵See that no one repays anyone evil for evil, but always seek to do good to one another and to everyone. ¹⁶Rejoice always, ¹⁷pray without ceasing, ¹⁸give thanks in all circumstances; for this is the will of God in Christ Jesus for you. (1 Thessalonians 5:14-18)

Pursue righteousness, godliness, faith, love, steadfastness, gentleness. ¹²Fight the good fight of the faith. Take hold of the eternal life to which you were called and about which you made the good confession in the presence of many witnesses. (1 Timothy 6:11b-12)

Take care, brothers, lest there be in any of you an evil, unbelieving heart, leading you to fall away from the living God. ¹³But exhort one another every day, as long as it is called "today," that none of you may be hardened by the deceitfulness of sin. ¹⁴For we have come to share in Christ, if indeed we hold our original confidence firm to the end. (Hebrews 3:12-14)

Therefore, since we are surrounded by so great a cloud of witnesses, let us also lay aside every weight, and sin which clings so closely, and let us run with endurance the race that is set before us, ²looking to Jesus, the founder and perfecter of our faith, who for the joy that was set before him endured the cross, despising the shame, and is seated at the right hand of the throne of God. (Hebrews 12:1-2)

But be doers of the word, and not hearers only, deceiving yourselves. (James 1:22)

Submit yourselves therefore to God. Resist the devil, and he will flee from you. ⁸Draw near to God, and he will draw near to you. Cleanse your hands, you sinners, and purify your hearts, you double-minded. (James 4:7-8)

But you are a chosen race, a royal priesthood, a holy nation, a people for his own possession, that you may proclaim the excellencies of him who called you out of darkness into his marvelous light. ¹⁰Once you were not a people, but now you are God's people; once you had not received mercy, but now you have received mercy. (1 Peter 2:9-10)

*Humble yourselves, therefore, under the mighty hand of God so that at the proper time he may exalt you, ⁷casting all your anxieties on him, because he cares for you. ⁸Be sober-minded; be watchful. Your adversary the devil prowls around like a roaring lion, seeking someone to devour. ⁹Resist him, firm in your faith, knowing that the same kinds of suffering are being experienced by your brotherhood throughout the world. ¹⁰And after you have suffered a little while, the God of all grace, who has called you to his eternal glory in Christ, will himself restore, confirm, strengthen, and establish you.
(1 Peter 5:6-10)*

*Do not love the world or the things in the world. If anyone loves the world, the love of the Father is not in him. ¹⁶For all that is in the world—the desires of the flesh and the desires of the eyes and pride of life—is not from the Father but is from the world. ¹⁷And the world is passing away along with its desires, but whoever does the will of God abides forever.
(1 John 2:15-17)*

Resources to Help You Pray for the Next Generation

A Father's Guide to Blessing His Children

A FATHER'S GUIDE TO
BLESSING HIS CHILDREN

Truth78

A blessing is a biblical way to express hope and vision for what a child will become. In one sense, it is a prayer asking God to make that hope and vision true for a child. It is also an opportunity to look a child in the eye and express your hope and vision for his or her life. The 29 blessings in this booklet provide a model for creating blessings of your own. Since each blessing is rooted in Scripture, this is another way to pray biblical prayers for your children and give them a biblical vision for their lives. As David Michael reflects on his experience as a pastor, father, and grandfather, he has witnessed more fruit from blessing others in this way than almost anything else he has done.

Praying for the Next Generation

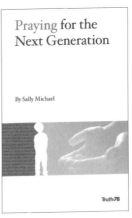

Praying for the Next Generation

By Sally Michael

Truth78

Using Psalm 1 as a guide, Sally Michael illustrates how to pray through a portion of Scripture. She also identifies 12 specific prayer topics with corresponding Bible passages to pray for your children and their children after them. This resource is recommended for pastors, children's ministry leaders and volunteers, as well as parents and grandparents—all who have a heart to pray for the next generation.

Utter Dependency on God, Through Prayer

The first part of *Utter Dependency on God, Through Prayer* is primarily directed to adults for their growth in the faith. The second part provides practical guidance to those who lead children in prayer—primarily in the classroom, but also in the living room. Eleven strategies for integrating prayer into your interactions with children will serve as a springboard for creative and visionary thought as you meditate on Scripture, seeking God with all of your heart, through prayer.

A Sure Foundation Nursery Curriculum

A Sure Foundation: A Philosophy and Curriculum for Ministry to Infants and Toddlers is designed to help you transform your ministry to infants and toddlers into an integral beginning—a place of prayer for young children, a place where they hear foundational Bible stories and simple Truth statements, and where they begin to memorize Scripture as they form their language skills. There is an emphasis on creating an environment of prayer for babies and strategically praying for each infant and toddler by name each time they are in your care.

The curriculum includes four stories for young toddlers (to be repeated throughout the year), 13 stories for older toddlers (ages 24-36 months) with monthly Scripture verses for them to memorize, and 16 stories with accompanying memory verses to use with toddlers 36 months and older until they graduate to a preschool Sunday school class.

Lord, Teach Us To Pray Intergenerational Curriculum

The purpose of prayer is not to change God, but to change the person praying. Through prayer, God reveals our sinful hearts, makes His will known, discloses His Kingdom purposes, and reveals Himself to His children. True prayer is getting to know God better. When Jesus responded to the disciples' request to teach them to pray, He gave them the Lord's Prayer as a model to show us what should be in the believer's heart when he comes to his Heavenly Father in prayer.

Lord, Teach Us To Pray: A Study for Children and Adults on Prayer is not about the correct formula for prayer—it's about God's children learning to fellowship with Him in prayer. This 13-week, intergenerational study on prayer is designed for Sunday school and midweek classes, church family nights, family nights at home, homeschool and Christian school settings, camps, and small groups. Small groups or families can work together through the Family Devotional Guide, which includes six days of devotional ideas per week.

About Truth78

Truth78 is a vision-oriented ministry for the next generations. Our vision is that the next generations know, honor, and treasure God, setting their hope in Christ alone, so that they will live as faithful disciples for the glory of God.

Our mission is to nurture the faith of the next generations by equipping the church and home with resources and training that instruct the mind, engage the heart, and influence the will through proclaiming the whole counsel of God.

Values that undergird the development of our resources and training are that they be God-centered, Bible-saturated, Gospel-focused, Christ-exalting, Spirit-dependent, doctrinally grounded, and discipleship-oriented.

Resources for Church and Home

Truth78 currently offers the following categories of resources and training materials for equipping the church and home:

Vision-Casting and Training

We offer a wide variety of booklets, video and audio seminars, articles, and other practical training resources that highlight and further expound our vision, mission, and values, as well as our educational philosophy and methodology. Many of these resources are freely distributed through our website. These resources and trainings serve to assist ministry leaders, volunteers, and parents in implementing Truth78's vision and mission in their churches and homes.

Curriculum

We publish materials designed for formal Bible instruction. The scope and sequence of these materials reflects our commitment to teach children and youth the whole counsel of God over the course of their education. Materials include curricula for Sunday schools, Midweek Bible programs, Backyard Bible Clubs or Vacation Bible Schools, and Intergenerational studies. Most of these materials can be adapted for use in Christian schools and education in the home.

Parenting and Family Discipleship

We have produced a variety of materials and training resources designed to help parents in their role in discipling their children. These include booklets, video presentations, family devotionals, children's books, articles, and other recommended resources. Furthermore, our curricula include parent pages to help parents apply what is taught in the classroom to their child's daily experience in order to nurture faith.

Bible Memory

Our Fighter Verses Bible memory program is designed to encourage churches, families, and individuals in the lifelong practice and love of Bible memory. The Fighter Verses program utilizes an easy-to-use Bible memory system with carefully chosen verses to help fight the fight of faith. It is available in print, on FighterVerses.com, and as an app for smart phones and other mobile devices. The Fighter Verses App includes review reminders, quizzes, songs, a devotional, and other memory helps. For pre-readers, Foundation Verses uses simple images to help young children memorize 76 key verses. We also offer a study, devotional guide, and coloring book that correspond to Set 1 of the Fighter Verses. Visit FighterVerses.com for the weekly devotional blog and for free memory aids.

Nonprofit Ministry

Truth78 is a 501(c)(3) nonprofit ministry structured to tell of "the glorious deeds of the LORD, and his might, and the wonders that he has done" (Psalm 78:4) to millions of children and youth in the next generation who do not know, honor, and treasure Jesus Christ. Ministry supporters make it possible to reach more children of the next generation globally through...

- Funding curriculum translation projects that we will distribute free through our website. We have resources in numerous languages. Major translation projects are completed for 16 languages, with 15 more underway.

- Providing free training materials to equip children's and youth ministry leaders, volunteers, and parents to develop a biblical vision for their ministry to the next generation, and to provide specific training on using our resources and on the roles and functions of children's and youth ministry.

- Underwriting a fund to help ministries and individuals unable to fully afford Truth78 resources.

For more information on Truth78 or any of these initiatives, contact:

Truth:78 / Equipping the Next Generations to Know, Honor, and Treasure God

Truth78.org
info@Truth78.org
877.400.1414
@Truth78org

HBBBEP